IN THE LANGUAGE OF LOST LIGHT

PATRICIA NELSON

Also by Patricia Nelson

Among the Shapes that Fold & Fly
Sugartown Publishing, 2013

Spokes of Dream or Bird
Poetic Matrix Press, 2017

Out of the Underworld
Poetic Matrix Press, 2019

Cover Art by Saundra Kiehn

Poetic Matrix Press
www.poeticmatrix.com

Credits

Grateful acknowledgement is made to the following periodicals in which these poems first appeared, sometimes in slightly different versions:

"Conquest" in *Califragile,* September 2018
"Parade" in *American Journal of Poetry*, January 2019
"Circles" and "Woman of Gray" in *The Pangolin Review*, January 2019
"Galahad" in *Panoplyzine*, Spring 2019
"The Day" in *Mojave River Review,* Spring/Summer 2019
"Merlin and Nimue" and "Intimations" in *Seventh Quarry*, July 2019
"Dream and Water" in *The Wild,* Marin Poetry Center Anthology 2019 (Ed. Jayne McPherson)
"Reflections" in *Abramelin,* 2019
"Avalon" in *Panoplyzine*, Fall 2019
"The Rose" in *Califragile*, October 2019
"Lancelot" in *Blue Unicorn*, Fall 2019
"Boy Stolen by Faeries" in *The Listening Eye,* October 2019
"The Dead" in *MockingHeart Review*, November 2019
"Arthur to Guinevere" and "Guinevere to Arthur" in *Rockvale Review*, November 2019
"The Sea at its Edge" in *Speckled Trout Review,* December 2019
"Mushrooms" in *Califragile,* Winter 2020
"Mythical Animal," "Island," and "Sight" in *Mojave River Review*, Spring 2020
"Those Who Have Been to the Fire" in *Mantis*, 2020
"Grief Song" and "What Word?" in *Seventh Quarry*, February 2020

"Prospero," "Garden," "The Other," "The Heavy Animals," and "A Place that Glows" in *Eunoia Review*, February 2020

"Where We Began" in *The Pangolin Review,* March 2020

"At the Top" and "Small Dangers" in *Hubbub*, 2020

"Another Vision" in *The Maynard, Spring,* 2020

"At the End" in *Big Windows Review*, May 2020

"Caliban," "Piccarda," and "Jupiter" in *. . . And Then,* Redwood Writers Anthology 2020 (Eds. Claggett and Bernstein)

"Adam: The First Language" and "The Language of Lost Light" in *Gyroscope Review,* Spring 2020

"Wish" in *California Quarterly,* Spring 2020

"The Monster" in *Mocking Heart Review,* June 2020

"Daedalus" and "Merlin the Tutor" in *Seventh Quarry*, July 2020

"Glaucus" in *The Courtship of Winds,* Summer 2020

"The Second Fall" and "In the Fable" in *Eunoia Review*, September 2020

"Witch" in *Bear Review,* Fall 2020

"Time and the Earthbound" in *Blue Unicorn,* Fall 2020

"Gawain" in *Transformation*, Marin Poetry Center Anthology 2020 (Ed. Sian Killingsworth)

"Icarus" and "When I Return" in *Beliveau Review,* November 2020

"Giant," "It Matters," "Vision of Paradise," and "The Nature of the Pageant" in *Lion and Lilac,* October 2020

"Why the Saints Are Quiet," "Hook for the Masterpiece," and "The Garden and the Thorns" in *Academy of the Heart and Mind,* September 2020

CONTENTS

IN THE LANGUAGE OF LOST LIGHT

THE GLOW OF AN EDGE

CAMELOT

PARADISO (AFTER DANTE)

Between The Worlds

About the Author

In the Language of Lost Light

THE GLOW OF AN EDGE

DAEDALUS

How clear it all seems now:
My child never understood,
never saw how I, the quiet watcher,
might see from a little height
what rises and what falls.

He never held the pale light
like a bowl of undulant milk,
lifted it slowly, without spilling it.
Never ignited the earth with sight,
the red apple and the dark road.

He saw no torrents in the sky,
nor the writhing of the candles.
Nor the small, subsidiary creatures
who nudge the dark carefully
with their soft and temporary flames.

He never loved the craft of seeing,
the sad largeness of its memory.
My hand: its willingness to hold,
still, extended like a dank tool,
even this empty sky.

ICARUS

i. The Rising

White-handed, leaning, loud,
he lifts and bulges like a sail.
His palm is full of sky.

He tries at first the middle wind:
a game of stillness—white gulls
floating in a silver light.

But there is hotter light above.
Light that rises like a roaring wave
and bares the creatures of the top.

His arms are whirlwinds,
avalanches, fists of light.
He wants to see and ride.

ii. The Visions

How clear it is in the fierce blue wind.
The twisting maze—solved. Its maker's
writhing soul appears like bright ink.

Even the monster begins to dim,
dissipates like noise in a dream
or dark lake. More a metaphor, a hint.

6

He sees creatures of the light.
He wants to speak—his lip widens
then forgets what it meant to name.

What gleam he meant to take
from the boiling cup of wishes
where the sad and the brave whirl.

iii. The Fall

Then the black and downward wind—
his shadow growing, large again
upon the rock and water, pulling him.

Air like a dream of falling,
blue horses strong and everywhere
who tear him with their anger.

This child with his wafting eye,
his loud and mis-aimed act
both wrong and not-wrong.

Wish

In its socket, the wish to fly insists,
loud, hard to unscrew from red air
rocking like a siren and a light.

The error rises and it flies.
It can do nothing else. In wanting,
there is only up and now and falling.

The shadow small and rising
from the rock below to meet you,
flying without air or plumage.

THE HEAVY ANIMALS

They walk on the stones,
those heavy, shade-throwing animals
with a beat of heat and cool.

The stones bear their closeness
and their tall apartness,
their noise, their breakage of sky.

Flying is simple
like a wish to be heard,
but out of reach for them.

They rehearse it in dream,
signing wildly
on air and distance.

Then they return to the daylight,
the difficult weight of their nature.
They drop like colors into the current,

Dissolving, changing the shade of everything.
A blue dye in the water, luminous,
one window floating in another.

DREAM AND WATER

With many turnings, water comes to the city
rising and falling in its joint of blue,
evangelist of a lost, cold purity.

Its silver light is left like a sorrow
in the cloud and high rock.

Nothing comes of purity
but dark and distance—

And then the mongrel light of morning
going everywhere, nudging, uncovering
what is new in the air and bright dirt.

PROSPERO

He calls the forces tethered
in the light like pale horses.
He is old among their voices.

In this final air he is music.
He shifts blue shoulders
and revises noise away.

He is indolent and simple.
A lizard on the rock, warm
in a slow, glowing ripple.

The old wildness is under him,
not quite of him anymore,
but like a spell he knows by heart.

Weariness is the last task.
It tugs on his boot with its height,
the last light on his mountain.

ARIEL

In the hole where I lay
with folded breath, I saw it:
a tall creature moved the dark.

I rose and glided like a spider,
a sticky silver spider in a ball of air.
Spiral, circle, toe. I rolled.

Of that moment, Prospero was king.
He painted the day like a sun.
Yellow-eyed toad, fat startled daisy.

I touched with my face the bright
white wind and I was a rant of light again,
a pot of blue and yellow weather.

Then I saw him weigh my soul.
He weighed it like an apple or a chicken.
Could he make it afraid again, and useful?

I don't hate a creature I can solve
or fit gently into the next wind.
That I can roll myself away from.

But I saw his eye and I remember it,
as the blue day holds for a moment
every damning thing.

And I am glad he's flown away
in his cloak of stolen light.

CALIBAN

i.
The forest puts a shimmer in its animals,
a binding root of light or want.
A green and tangled dreaming.

Then those others came, talking animals
who floated loudly out of the edge of the world
on the splotches of their books and grievances.

They could not find the wordless things,
black noises in the trees, flying lights,
all that was caught or stilled there—

Those visitors in their ranks and coverings.
I mimed what hid from them. Bright things.
The things I loved. Betrayers!

ii.
The forest mostly loves its creatures,
rolls them in light and dark and yellow,
birds who live in a space that flickers.

It flies their colors in the summer
when the river rattles. Colors that will sleep
when the forest smells moon or the white winter.

I think the forest loves my eye, my silver eye
in its furry, weeping slot. Its veer and sway,
the way it shakes excitement out of empty air.

The way it knows the colors, the temporary gibber
of the light. That's the view I understand
and must call beautiful and true. Must love.

iii.
I gave them all I knew, so quickly, shuffling
as if dancing with the height I saw in them,
the strange brightness of the air around them.

They took it and forgot me. They laughed
and I saw myself as if for the first time: ugly.
One of the creatures that spit and slide

Along the afterlight, a daub, a blot
that swims briefly when the lamp goes out.
A dark thing living in light by sufferance.

It is they who should hide.
They should scuttle in the light,
crawl like fire on a black wick.

For I have seen who they are.
Let them live there. Let them
rattle like a pile of scorpions.

ISLAND

There is light at the brink of a sea
or a fall or a death by knowledge.
Any edge where you are stopped
from continuing as you are.

You walk on the brightness of sand.
You—a heaviness that moves.
An aching of soles proceeding
on a thing you cannot keep.

The wave eats the quiet beach.
Stand upon that winnowing
like a wish without a word
for what it wants next.

THE SEA AT ITS EDGE

The sea is full of illusion.
Thoughts move in swells
as far and blue as islands.

Light is near it like the rain.
The deeps of our words swim here.
We remember how things happened.

The island blue and lost is not a loss,
only a difficult change of distance.
Harsh like the strangeness of birds.

THE OTHER

When you come to the edge,
lean your ear. Name and drop
an image still as glass:
the thing that you are not.

Listen to its falling.
It curves, it swims,
a mote of mirror.
Float in its silver.

Let its brightness pull
the rope lying in your dream
like a light coiled downward,
glowing with what it wants.

The Other will move toward you,
fly out of silence like an owl.
A thump, a sudden eye,
yellow and black and wide.

THE SECOND FALL

i.
This is the desert of patience and perspective.
It shimmers with stars and misdirection.
Implies to silver skin that rain might come.

Colors move in their different speeds,
some beating and sweating, some not.
Colors of mule and rock and scorpion.

In such a place the souls might gather
after death or after a fall.
A fall that holds a piece of flying.

ii.
Far away, the wet beginning of the world:
the coming together, the curving
murmuring its creatures small and tidal.

The gray fish that won't come again
bending the rains and salts and grasses.
The pale-eyed birds.

They came without thought or prompting,
animals as repetition and revision
and the resounding of voices.

Every animal you named is gone.
Their echo is—and is gone.

PARADE

In the beginning is joy,
the dance with its gunfire stepping.
The joinder of many: greed, anger,
fast hearts tripping and falling.

Words rip as marchers go by
in a swing of glove and boot.
The crowd plays sticks and tubes,
hoots the tuneless song of largeness.

They come from beyond and away.
They swing their voices like confetti.
They make the noise and the parade
that will go on without them.

There are moments like corners
where the many stop and look up,
press small breaths against the sky,
the large and ancient stars.

GARDEN

Oh lips and lops and women
in the middle of their shadows
walking wide by wide.

They are stopping
by the yellow, loosened roses,
lean on the roundness of air.

Oh they seem to blow,
rise and widen,
ride the colors like a breath.

Oh they talk with their little wrists
of wisps and wasps,
the hot, whittled light.

The end of the day is scented
and stated loudly on the gravel
in their long, wide shadows.

Colors that move imply a softness.
All of it curves and has a side,
a blue light on a bubble.

But they infer
with their sliding eyes
a fall, with breakage.

A pop, a bang, a gavel, and all the skies
and all the eyes go on without them,
empty for a little while.

THOSE WHO HAVE BEEN TO THE FIRE

Those who have been to the fire
come back walking the ledge,
walk loose in a coat and a shadow.

They move slowly like the shade
toward what they know of home
and the light of its new strangeness.

They bear in their skin
the known openings,
the sentient ear and scar.

Is it loss or is it beauty: the change
that fastens at the window's edge
quietly, like a spider's silver wish?

SMALL DANGERS

Fall asleep with your gray-blue
thoughts upon the small calamities.
The square rattle of a window, say,
a little falling and a rocking view.

Don't dream about the larger edge,
the ledge that sees everything.
The weathers that blow you
to the hotter, meaner places.

Don't think your way to the myth.
The hell that is tall with flowers,
painted fires, winds with mouths,
bright wounds exhaling.

Don't name the bigger fear.
Let it flicker in a shadow.
Keep two eyes on the middle.
Let your dreams carry what is little.

AT THE TOP

It's narrow at the top.
Something mythical rustles,
some pale animal
spotted like a page.

And a white wind goes,
broken in the black trees
singing its particular,
hungry loss.

Some climb up the shiny top
and love it with a child's joy,
roll loudly down the hill
like a bottle of light.

Some fly toward a sky
as thin and sticky as a web.
Put skin to a shape they cannot see:
the cry, the fierce wonder.

In the Fable

One character exemplifies restraint,
his shadow touches the world,
not heavily, not pulling on the air.

One character comes from the land of the dead.
He is made of organs again, and joy. Bird-loud,
tilting at the small specks nearest to his eye.

The last is love, the instrument one taps
or blows upon with skill and memory.
She makes a music that is quiet at first
like starlight. A far thing.

She requires translation and a warning:
The face of your transformation is cool
and white, small enough to enter the world
but it is hot at the source and roars.

Like the day, she changes the fragrance,
makes the jasmine's white scent smaller,
dimmer than it was in the night
like a belief she has feasted upon.

WITCH

—The witch speaks to Hansel and Gretel

How gladly you forgot it all, how easily
the flutter of light around me went away,
the chittering forest of the fairy tale.

First my fingers, then my crooked steps,
then the glances knotted with a hook. How I stood
with my nose upwind of all the crying.

You forgot the copse with odd things
at its border, thorns and edges, itching and stinging—
and also the soft dark wandering dream.

The dream that holds the circling things,
the round swarm, the dancer, the wheel.
The bend and the edge. The dream that warns.

You'll find that edge again, your own wish to devour
with hand and eye whatever you thought you wanted.
Your fists will lengthen like thirsty shadows.

You'll see again the strange, collapsing light,
confusion filling the space like birds,
your eyes twisting as you fall through the dark.

26

You who cannot help but scatter
in your dreams, your tattered stories,
the winking trail, the crumbs of light.

They allow me to see you still,
to be suddenly close like the smell of rain,
the small dark circles one upon the other.

The color of ghost
that is suddenly everywhere,
more permanent than you.

CAMELOT

ARTHUR

How heavy on its stem my dream
of love seems now, a season of color
fabricating apples out of mindless weather.

It is place as much as memory,
a small, bright river where I held everything
in the rushing slenderness of sight.

Her eye was the blue of morning,
dreamt by cold, bright water.
A forgetting of all that contradicts.

A place where the hour narrows
and sands go faster, brighter, as if fated.
A gleam in the wind and in my hand.

Love is denser when it loses this,
smaller as the heart is after fear—
A dull thing that resists,

An undertow that stirs the motes,
bright creatures whirling
toward the cold white sturgeon.

ARTHUR TO LANCELOT

How young it was, our oath
where the right words seemed to live,
the right acts in their own air.

It isn't rage I feel now, or sorrow only,
but a wind like a sound repeating.

A song that knew its notes
before they gathered, and loved them.
Loves them still.

We held the music like a palm and fingers
on a gate, as if we were folding a distance.

Then the knowing vanished like a sound
and we heard the random voices.

Those who hated us danced
in their low and yellow light,
their foolishness,
laughing with their hanging mouths.

Arthur to Guinevere

i.
If I had loved you more—
or loved the hound-smooth task
of baying toward your beauty
in a story's spotted light—

If I'd looked farther into you, or longer
in the little, sudden room
where you were mine and full of colors
like the sunlight or an easy gift—

The flames would not have come for you,
or the mean and lurching truth,
the light from the hot, white fire
of what you are not.

ii.
You were a pang of starlight,
farther than my understanding.
You were a truth that now has gone,
leaving a story—a sad and lesser thing.

You do not love me as the story does.
And there's a different light around you—
a meanness flickering, thickening like snow.

I hold duty now: its heaviness, its strange density.
A still, gray stone that I will hold
until I am empty and covered with cold.

Until I too am without thought
and beautiful. A story.

LANCELOT

Beauty pulled me with its calm.
It came over me like morning,
a sky full of time and clarity
and cold as a lake.

I fell first and most fiercely there,
into her tranquil air. How steeply
I blundered into my vacant soul,
both grateful and unaware of falling.

Thoughts arrived that shook the path,
the way I had come, the prayer of the story.
Words began to bang like large animals,
striped and splotched, inarticulate.

And suddenly the love was out,
beyond the broken fence.
A running of weights and odors
that knew their way (but not all of it).

That air darkened suddenly,
like a canyon, when the lines fell.
When others came with their claims,
watchers glimmering in waves around us.

They come to gloss the story
as it ricochets, to disprove the wild colors
loosened and crowing like parrots.
To sing to me of distance—age or ripeness.

I saw, as I lost, the thing with height, taller
than the eye goes with its small blue,
its judging and rescuing,
into the place where all is visible.

GUINEVERE TO ARTHUR

i. The Beginning

The wizard warned you away from me!
His pale mouth sagged.
His face slackened like a dead thing.
His soul was oddly visible to me,
its sad and dying light.

I was red with rage, lion-bright.
I—who flared among your enemies.
I—the light that danced for you.
Strode into fire for you as if it were music!

Not an idea! Not a portent or a curse!
And never your downfall,
the one who unraveled it all!

More a mild animal that loved you,
loved the wish that lies in love.

A muscular, innocent thing
like a tail or an eyeball
that moves utterly when it is pleased
and eager to follow.

I was wide-faced, loud.
I wiped the world with my grin.

Many men are crooked in the light,
but I saw you straight and clear.
My love floated, white buds dropping.
I wanted you to see it as it was. Aglow!

ii. The End

I wanted to make us the same,
two lights turning like pages,
touching one wind.

I wanted you to look at me,
wanted it with the red-faced fervor
of a washerwomen, dragging a thing through lye,
knowing what it needed to be.

I can almost touch the sorcerer's words.
His truths that hardened around me,
began to glow gradually, like minerals,
covering me with a strange light.

I raise my arms with knots and knuckles
at the end. Their odd entanglement
in all that was lost, their several nearnesses.

I arrive at a death, many deaths.
The woman writhing in a lie,
words that allowed me to love
and not love, to love elsewhere.

Let me go among the corrupt,
the dead with their ash-white eyes.
Let the singers blow
on the little fire of what I meant.

TRISTRAM

I don't fear the shadow
or the dusk's cold glow.
But here I hesitate, grow still
in a sky thick as marrow.

My forehead creases
and is bright, like water.
I am not at ease.

It all comes back to me:
the voyage to Ireland,
the light on the river,
the gleams of air among the firs.
So ordinary, so soft and accidental.

My task was the gliding woman.
To guide the potion and the boat.
To go upon the river like an oil,
or a dream, touching nothing.

The task was a cloth
that made me blank. And beautiful.

It was there the error came
and deepened like the water.
changed the river like a trick of light.

It's not the bitter vial I remember now.
It's the liquid of a dream—
her hair still sudden there,
still widening like a yellow spill.

My soul saw beauty all at once,
fluttered like a sparrow into speech.
Thoughts went everywhere like ants
feeling for the bottom of that sweetness,

I know the words of honor,
the gleam as they flow among trees,
and the white-robed kings,
but I will never hold that light again.

GALAHAD

i.
The grail was moon or wilderness
I saw it as through a glass
green after green, a forest translucent.

My thread to mend the dark,
a light my eye could follow.

The path moved like water as I
crossed it with the other riders.
The path was high and strange,
hushed as in an eclipse.

ii.
I turned my eye to the stars.
I did not look when monsters
twisted in the corners,
when the story folded back on itself.

Belief was the line in the dark,
a light I followed down the road.
The road that is made of mind
and other dangers.

The grail white as moonlight
a circle seen from many places,
wearing silence and an arc.

ii.
The grail was a distant star for some,
floating, burning and unsafe,
sometimes below the line of the eye,
never the same in its consequences.

For me it never changed.
Is that the same as goodness?
To look away when the story fades,
revising the tokens of bright and dark?

iii.
I live on in what is real,
exuding music, a discarded symmetry.
I feel the grail still, an image like silk,

Like silence on my fingers
when the sky is dark
and tall and I remember I'm alone.

When the loss of my companions
is larger than my love for the grail.

They say I will live forever
in this sadness without further instructions.

GAWAIN

*—Gawain's strength waxed and waned with
the sun. One of the greatest knights of the Round
Table, he was never compromised by ambiguous
acts or conflicted emotions.*

The enemy is beautiful to me,
the monster that makes me strong.
The sun is beautiful that comes with heat and light,
days that roll with roaring, sea-tall ogres.

And honor, that old swaying bell
is beautiful though it is heavy as a cow,
spotted and awkward and stinking
of all the things that have moved it.

Though it moves slowly in its sounds,
though it sees and calmly eats the faithful,
still it is beautiful in its indifference,
its call that tells me what I am, what I must do.

The Act is a prayer, not of wanting
but of transformation, a song for the loss
or change of the self. A love of the useful monster.
A bell of fire-bright veins.

MORGAN REMEMBERS

From the blue of a bog
the vision unwinds:
a shining, improbable horse,
a long, awkward man.

Arthur, holding his wishes
like untidy roses.
Like a color that opens
the odor of light.

My brother, in the glow
some dreadful angel made—
made it out of boredom
or because he could—
twisting it into a world
that doesn't love it.

Once he was smaller, nearer.
A child with glimmering fears,
and tall bright enemies.
A boy in a sky so high and gray
it shook with strangeness.

A fragile boy who could not help
but whisper to the light.
And to every thing that flickers
longing onward like a river.

MERLIN THE TUTOR

They occupy a booming summer,
faces new as leaves and upward,
these children who will grow into age
like a costume, an enchantment.

They rest like hands as I talk of magic.
Not surprised if I draw oddities on the world.
A world where every shadow demonstrates
the mutable size of light and time.

Boys don't chill or darken in the magic,
the little task that touches and slightly rearranges them.
They wear an occasional strangeness on their skin
like freckles or the temperature of the shed.

I blow light upon the strengths they need.
Calm light like a moon where small holes drift.
Or the visions: sudden, a lightning showing
the silence of dead souls on the battlefield.

Days drop from the horizon, burn like blue boulders.
Winters: cold ground, small comet-colored light.
Summers bringing fire and war, the squawk of territory,
men like stiff-legged jays—men they must meet.

I will go with them fading like a shadow.
Every battle, every death, holding the child's
straight and silver wish to know. And still I insist,
with a love like the vacant, wailing water.

MERLIN AND NIMUE

—Merlin was a magician who lived backward in time, growing younger and losing knowledge as time passed. He fell in love with Nimue, who prevailed on him to teach her his magic. She tired of Merlin and used his own magic to imprison him under a stone.

i.
She was beautiful, resting in her time.
Summer stalking forward in a hide
as temporary and as blatant as a leopard's.

All that is beautiful and spotted, wafted
like an odor, a flower's yellow scent.
She was almost comic in her trickery, operatic.

She could have come in duller colors,
a black hood signaling her malice.
Her fear of the devil she held in her heart.

But she came singing, holding a stone to hide me.
A weight the color of ash—meant to deceive.
She came bearing the absence of light.

ii.
Now I am the darkened whale,
pocked and bitten like the moon,
waiting to breathe the light again.

A stone is a space folded back on itself,
a love or knowing folded,
folded many times until it is heavy.

Perhaps I held some magic back from her.
Or maybe I have had enough of air—and beauty.
Perhaps I will be the air, or beauty.

I might wash myself in another form
and come to her when she is old and bitter
with air around me and a blue light.

Morgan to Arthur

i.
The winds are sewn to your shoulders:
Motifs whistling the breadth,
the folds of your way forward.

The airy cloth of fate and magic:
Birds not wholly bound
to what is true or what is level.

And your god who calls you upward
with his twining voice,
he too is not of the level world.

His love is a fall of pale leaves
among the stiff, black canes. A gleam
whereby the old ways are revised away.

His forgiveness random as a wand, and fretful.
Grace, a little scented light—clouds
that blow away like fat gray roses.

ii.
I live in a place where wrongs are real
and remembered, and forgiveness
is a beating thing of string and bone.

My air holds what lives there, all your veering
chattering kings. They throb like a rising of bats.
They are long at the fingers and they squeak.

Who is your God to pardon them, who are you?
The whole world aches of your destiny,
the light from my shattered season.

Your thieving god is far and tall and cold,
but small and near are those who love Him.
Those who wronged me with their hot lies.

They are mine.

Arthur Is Dead

Change is marked in the stones.
The kingdom alters like a dune—
soil adrift with small creatures,
dreams that moan.

Where will Arthur go, unfastened
from his story, the weight of our love?
Will we know him again?
Will other kings come in colder colors?

The kingdom's sleepers dream of flying.
Dream that loss is a winter they will outlast.
That light can rot like flowers and grow back.
A fall of blue particles passes over them.

What did the lost light mean, that spills
black wishes and white ashes?

MORGAN ON MAGIC

I felt his death on my skin. Arthur
going elsewhere like a warm wind.

I wanted to touch the loss
with my hands and voice.

To cry in the vowels I dream in
which lift and migrate like the birds.

I wanted to carry him in my eyes.
to lead him home
gently, like a glowing animal.

And to curse the mute white sky,
swell like the loud black bees.
To slide like the red worm
writing in the apple.

To cast a spell: What is magic
but small flying words
that caw at what they can't undo?

Magic must lean fiercely
over the soft unborn, fold them
in the light of what is broken,
the wounds that will alter
and say something else.

AVALON

Circle of soil closed to plow or prayer
but sowing the scent of grass and apples
everywhere and upward, like a story of flying.
A flowering as brilliant as the spotted horses,
a season leaning forward—wilder than joy.

The sealed place of glass and mist,
waves in which the recent dead, like eagles,
feed or float. The sad and silver dead,
kneaded by magic and battle,
not yet wholly estranged from healing.

And the lake: a blue wheel whirling
with its axis elsewhere, in another kind of time.
Lobes of motion and cold that glitter for a moment
on one fable, one imperfect, sorrowing hero
who wears well his hour and his sword.

Water is a sentience tended by women.
Images green and gliding on the top
and below, what is real and hard to see:
a weapon or a task that sinks and shimmers,
always deeper and more difficult.

The Unbiddable Women of Avalon

Do our spells frighten you?
Anger your favorite god
alive in a flap of shadow?

The light of a spell appears
when we sing and turn a wheel,
weave the white tent of our love.

The light is old, ambiguous.
It is stone or the color of stone
ablaze on the cold side of a mountain.

It can mend a tired king,
send him back, glowing
with hardship and our love.

Return him to those who love him
with the weight of mountains.
People he must disappoint.

A spell we sing must spend his light,
his white light floating like a sleeve.
We cannot weave a waiting spell.

We cannot call some shining beast
with silver hoof and a mythical horn
that will carry him on its hair

To a task that loves him as he is
in a world implausibly bright—
a world still windless and unspoiled.

That is a weather beyond us
and far beyond a muttered spell.

MORDRED

> —*Mordred was the ambitious, envious half-brother who brought down King Arthur's reign. Legend says that Arthur will return from the dead to rule Britain again.*

i.
I come on a huffing horse
and dust the color of lamplight:
Mordred alive in a wheel of air,
done with the dim and moaning dead.

I am thin and loose as the bear in spring.
And it is I the prophecy returns
in a season that rises like an odor of blood.

The world is around me, the tools of light
that I touch freely like an apple or an axe
though I am not of the light myself.
I am king.

Not tall Arthur, white and sweating
in his metals. Arthur caught
in the bright paw of his light.

ii.
Perhaps I'm not quite as I was
when I first occupied the world.
When I died of envy and a yellow wound.

The colors are strange:
Air that holds its blue above me.
And this red that is not quite red?
It swirls and burns like iodine,
dyes the world like an uncanny sun.

But enough of that. I say it is beautiful—
beautiful enough—to have breath again.

We will see who is stronger,
Mordred or this eerie light.

INTIMATIONS

There is light in the trees,
a clear sound that is everywhere.
The day twists, and we twist, waiting
for the light to scratch us open like a seed.

The glasses here hold the dark drink
with points of light, an ivy of lights,
and we swallow gladly
the sticky dance of light and dark.

We move at first on our lightness,
our joints of silk, and when the jolts come
palm or knuckle move without thought
to the grass below or the pane of a door.

There is the strangeness of color
like a scent of somewhere else.
All at once the world of the dead is nearer.
What is real comes over us like morning.

THE MONSTER

The air is bright and soft as pollen.
Then a different kind of shine,
heat and dark and sound that glows.

Something else, something nearer,
mutters in the bottom of the weather.
The monster—here to try the world again.

He rubs our summer with his yellow eye,
moves the air around our skin,
the lushness in which we hide.

He is bold, he rolls on what we love
as if it had an odor and a shape.
He wants what we want, clearly.

We make the words that rise against him,
bent and many-eyed like insects.
We—the bright-handed beasts with prayers.

The noise that says we love
the summer's purple flowers,
the warm white rain of light.

PARADISO
(AFTER DANTE)

PICCARDA

—Dante meets an acquaintance in Paradise: Piccarda, whose brother forced her to leave a convent for a marriage that advanced her family's fortunes. Dante wonders why this places her in the lowest circle of Paradise, farthest from God.

i.

He's gone, the brother who stole me
for the hot world, deployed me there.
Gone, the power in his hand
like a caliper, a narrow insect.

Gone, the marriage I entered
like a poppy lying down
in the wind I knew
was bright and lethal.

I did not refuse.
I wore obedience. And fear.
I did not love with heat or nearness.
Not the world, not my God.

I almost loved the distance,
the music of apartness.
The thoughts that play in hearts
where certain strings are silenced.

ii.
A small woman, soft shape,
hands upward like blossoms
staving off or ceding.

A little, fragrant sigh. I was dreamt,
a little wind of pale petals
pleasing for a while to someone.

A wind of dying, floating butterflies.
The dying and diminishment
inconsequential, as I was.

iii.
I set aside the rose-white veil,
tearing my vow—the one I made
in a place I thought was cool and gentle.

You ask me: did I grieve
my softness and my coolness,
the loss of my vehement God?

I have eyes of mirror and water here.
I wade in the colors of moon
and distance. My colors.

This is what I am, a glow
that holds its white breath
among the taller, hotter stars.

I do not grieve the God
who made me willow
to the stream of light.

IT MATTERS

It matters how a women is lost,
how her first intention falls
and rises somewhere else.

How the fault can travel
like a color or a cloud
into the death that re-envisions it.

How she untangles the dark, lifts it
by its edges so that even the breakage
has a wholeness and a light.

REFLECTIONS

They are weightless,
vaporous as words.
Only their faces move
like shapes on water.

They who left the world crudely,
as heat that enters the black seam,
the explosive wheel of dust—
to become this other thing
so slow and so clear.

They see the circle of the air:
a rim where yellow lions pause.
White flowers bright at dusk
and at the edge of sight.

They own the wind's transparency
wield like bells the sky's strength.

CIRCLES

—Dante envisions Heaven as a hierarchy of
revolving circles based on proximity to God.

Is it less to be outside the circle
that turns faster, closer to the Light?
Outside the wall—the bright, burning one?

To know Light by your difference,
the candle low at the flame, light
rustling like the small, new leaves?

To come cool or late to the truth,
to praise the middle shapes,
the slow, gray sermon of the shadow?

Is it sad to wait for light like a pool
in the ash-white day?
To shake the color of moon?

To be the pale flower
that is vivid only in the dark?
The "everywhere" in "God is everywhere"?

The Nature of the Pageant

It isn't real: There is no parade,
no ranking of the dead who rise
from the ground like daffodils.

The pageant is spectacle,
foolish approximation.

Hangs lights as thick as lemons
on the crudeness of your senses.
It touches you with roundness
and a small heaviness.

It is music, an error made
with beautiful instruments.
The intent of the deception softer
than your own voice. More conditional.

It suggests the blue that flies
beyond your simple bluebirds.

WHY THE SAINTS ARE QUIET

Home is a primal wind.
It rocks as the willows do
or the round womb.
The saints have found it.

They have touched
the moon-smooth thread
that asks for stillness and gives light.

They move as the pliant clouds do,
white with memory.

The saints are calm in Heaven,
sway in its sky like weather.
They know why they are there.

The saints are still
when the stars come close.
The stars remember them
like the scent-filled noses of animals.

JUPITER

The middle is where I am and how I see.
A place between two colors, two temperatures:
the red of Mars and Saturn's cold white mirror.

I sit in the chair of equal distance,
judging. There are children there
who love the patient helix of my ear.

I hear the little wind of their voices.
I am the tree that breathes the dark
and makes for them a small white flower.

A boy touches the ancient green of a frog
and knows with his hot, smooth hand
the way the colors jump in the world.

GLAUCUS

—Dante compares himself to Glaucus, a mythical
fisherman who placed his catch on a shore and saw
the fish magically revive. Glaucus ate some of the
grass on the bank and was seized with a longing
for the sea. He swims into the sea and becomes one
with the sea gods.

I have entered Paradise
like the gaping fish
that wakes and walks on sand.

Like Glaucus who ate the grass
where the magic fish had lain
and swam like a god through the sea.

I too bend toward the miracle,
the wave, the blue so wild
I believe in its sea of angels.

I glide among undulant saints.
I move the curve of my forehead
following their shine.

I brighten as I leave behind
the place I knew. I widen
like a violet into the sea's blue.

For I have eaten like an herb
the strange language of light
and I have seen many changes.

I who am arrogant and vain
begin to speak simply,
to think in small questions.

ADAM: THE FIRST LANGUAGE

—*When Dante meets Adam in Paradise, he asks him what the first language was. He also learns that Adam's real sin was impatience, not waiting to receive the whole knowledge that God intended to give him when he was ready.*

First language? My impatience.
All the things that vanished
when I came swinging my voice.

I went among the creatures
like eyes desiring their wildness,
their strange loneliness.

Naming was the gate
they had to pass through
in the singleness I could see.

I rose like the owl's moon mask.
One by one I snatched
their little cries of light.

Bright gusts of air
beautiful to me
as waves or sunsets.

One day I died too.
My words blew away like bones.
The world was new again.

LANGUAGE OF LOST LIGHT

> —Dante posits that when Adam and Eve fell from
> Paradise, the light broke and was scattered in pieces
> into the world, like pages of a book.

Can I call back shattered light
blown singing into the world?
The song is torn, scattered
like the page-white birds.

Follow the chittering ovals
over the trees and into the wind
on wings the color of sand.

They are shadows.
The meaning moves.
The sum of each is small.

Can I find the whole again,
the light that is full of memory?
The way past this blue light,
this lovely flying breakage?

SIGHT

i.
I will forget the gliding light,
the light that holds angels,
I will try to breathe it.

I will try to hold the glow
with hands that do not glow.
The light that sees me
as nothing human sees.

But I will fall back
through the smaller, dimmer images.
Images that speak of light
as battle or anomaly,
if it is spoken of at all.

ii.
The world has beauties,
clues to the light:
Nights of hay and moon
where yellow returns at morning
on the edge and curve.

Where the scent of hay dims
as day birds lift and small
beautiful creatures move in the leaves
and grass as we forget them.

A Place that Glows

On my path I will come to
the place I know and do not know.
The radiance that lies in my dreaming
like the heat of a scarlet reptile.

I will own the colors that open
there, the brevity of the lights
that stripe the day like butterflies.

Will touch the green air of the river
and feel something slow and level,
a swan-bright line.

I will know it when it gleams ahead
and is also somehow in my hand,
which I will lift in recognition
like a lantern weeping visions.

TIME AND THE EARTHBOUND

Earthbound creatures know it well,
the strict and blue horizon,
the circle that turns.

They who are mortal, who return in dream
to the nondescript window of the act
to look upon its size and meaning.

To pour facts over its smallness,
a slant of salt or color—or bitter time
to make the mind remember and compare.

To recall small oddities, the many colors
of grasses coming like an upward rain
to cool them, though that is not the task of colors.

To bring to the act their sadness, their love.
To gather with their two-colored eyes
the last daylight, like a river moving what is visible.

They carry like a stone the sky above them,
odd-colored, heavy, and personal
because it is full of time.

THERE IS NO TIME HERE

Do they understand this hush,
the space like a still, blue point
untangling sky and music?

They who see the seam of the horizon
where stars and meaning drain
and recall only what has vanished there.

They want to be apart from time,
live where the objects glow forever
and move like the belling wind.

They want to fall over the edge
and dance like the tamping bees
on the scent of everything at once.

THE ROSE

i.
How, but by forgetting, can I leave
the yellow glow of the center,
the white rose raveling beauty?

I brighten even in its shadow
but must turn earthward now,
graying like a cloud.

The rose still floats in my skin
like an image riding on a river,
which the river does not see
and cannot help but change.

ii.
I go among tenants of the earth.
They are full of dark.
Creatures like the hardness of a wall.
Harder after nearness to the stars.

I grow colder, dimmer,
lift the little human lamps
that tug like yellow beaks
at what they cannot know.

I open the story of the rose,
loving the hearers as I was loved.
Loved by the light that saw me striving.
Saw my errors near me: bird strikes with a dead glow.

I brush the story with the truth
until I seem sad and foolish—as indeed I was.
The fool who imagines one can call the light
and carry the white rose home.

WHEN I RETURN

What do I say of my vision
and its thinning tail of light?
Do I dream a house to hold it
with love and small black nails?

Say my days grew thick as snow,
shook me like a loud white wind?
That I was falling when the light came,
knew me with its nose like a wolf?

That it lay its warmth near me, its eye?
That my soul accelerated toward it
like the last thing loosened?
Does that fierce light live here?

There is only the gull that folds
a white line as a world slides under it.
The fountain that lifts its brightness,
tosses the weight of water like an apple.

And there is the odd warm light
that stays on my palms:
whiteness rising like the dawn
where unexplained stars float.

Between The Worlds

THERE IS SOMETHING

The sky lets out its sounds,
its small colors, its weathers.
Some are blue as birds,
glide among us like a light.

But there is something else—
a cold hole in the brightness,
an eddy of old knowledge.
It moves quickly like the river.

Something just beyond the shimmer
slides deeper, as if covering a tail,
a foot, and then the transparent odor.

The striped and yellow dawn resounds
like the hair of an animal
once everywhere but now rare.

Vision of Paradise

Someone is ill and dreams
a gray and fern-soft wind:
the swaying weather of Heaven.

The light of the dream is cool,
holds pale fog and black rock,
moves like the odor of lilies.

The light falls everywhere,
calls animals into bright air.

Animals with shadows that swing,
touching the curve of the animal
and the dark wave of the earth.

Legless animals that slide,
lay long shapes in the dust.

Wolves with oval mouths
pull the undulant moon close.

That's the way things move
in Heaven. Everything sways
and everything stays.

Another Vision

It's a different place without the fever dream:
The salvation slow and awkward, the sinners
loud and heavy, hauled out of the dark
like buckets, banging on the rocks.

The haulers complain, swinging the blackness
of their mouths, their eyes that glitter
weakly like broken stems or spigots.
In this Paradise, stars roll like wreckage.

Blossoms twist like knuckles stiffened
by the hard task, the cold of the tools.
The monster in the shadow doesn't growl
or poke your hiding places with its fingers.

No, it has a tall, gold eye that counts
and loves, but only as is due,
showing you the hardness of the truth.
And it speaks to certain devils in Hell:

The little ones as curious as gerbils,
who scamper lightly over the damned,
touching their intentions,
leaving a dread as soft as hands.

THE DAY

The day is small that bares
the women with bright sleeves,
the swish of temporary grasses,

The flare of apple that comes
from the circle of stem and rot,
revising both, making them sweet.

The day is deep with failed animals.
A wilderness of extinct objects
returned to their fading sockets.

Unseen eons shift as the day returns.
The insult ripens like a clotted web.

WHERE WE BEGAN

It might be blue, a blue that sees.
But is it beautiful and tall?
Single-minded like the heron
with its yellow, tilted eye?

Like a thumb that counts the spaces
and then quickly slides a bead?
A ripe red moon that wipes the world
with other creatures and an odder light?

Does the sum remember what we lost,
the dead who fell away like ashes?
Is it silent, is it true, as they are,
aghast in their different light?

Can a blue beginning hold
the weight of all this fading heat,
the ghost noise in the brush
when something warm and wary passes?

Red Embryo

Don't touch with thoughts
this tide with something
swimming out of it
that lives by ear and lip.

The object in its veiny echo
has already changed.
It is resting now,
finished like a sum.

Pulled out of nothing,
wrapped in lines, a body:
a way into the world
and a way out.

HOMUNCULUS

It waits with me at the first door,
soft, unfinished, silent as dough.
Fat and simple as a snowman,
it apes and mocks me with its sway.

It wants to harden and become serviceable,
to go with me into the contagious dancing.
Its wish is cruder, more persistent
than the writhing shadow at my heel,

It holds me in the wistful holes of its eyes,
strews my dark shape on the rocks.
Makes accidental art as it folds my image
with its pale hands, sometimes beautifully.

Or perhaps it makes a joke: This thing that saw
me go among the sufferers without flinching
or remembering much—as they don't flinch for me
but mostly take a small and mean advantage.

At the end, will it come again like a little tune?
Will it dance at last, turn an unforgiving eye?
Will it remember me, still unfinished
in my little white house dissolving
in the fiercer light of the moon?

Boy Stolen by Faeries

For me there is no way back.
In my place beyond the door I dream
of many things: the weather in the womb,
a tiny light, the wild shape of time.

The way my mother held me,
one who had just arrived in reality:
Held my smallness in her hands,
held the tallness still to come.

She loved my mild eyes, the skin
that seemed to tie me to the pale air of home.
She didn't see I would have wandered anyway
into the tricks of light.

My soul has room for something shriveled
and dissembling. A thing craving both
the mildness of milk and freedom,
but craving freedom more.

I went with a gulping eye and willingly
to live in a place where every light
is known to be a trick, a place for doubt.
I love to dance in its tangled tune.

I look from there through the cold
green mirror of your dreaming
and all your gentle loves.

WOMAN OF GRAY

Night rattles like a hedge
when she mutters and pushes in.
She moves by foot and finger
in a tangle of black edges.

The woman with a seam of light
and eyes as bright as thorns.
Her hands fill with cold
and the moon's white lament.

She bears the warm wind
she has always carried on her back.
The sky that unravels,
rains on her as slowly as the stars.

It floats her in a white sea.
toward those misplaced others
fastened like shadow to her memory
and the waterline of words.

A glow in which she isn't wholly lost.

AT THE END

If something still remains of me, and wakes
when earth or fire slides the animal away,
what then?

Do I dwindle in a smaller, thinner air?
Do I keep my memory of skin
where the new light touches me like wind?

Will the sky be white
with objects that move gently
as a fall of snow or pages, pleasing me?

Will there be colors and a sun?
Small birds on straight and blooming lines,
eyes leveled, staring outward?

Or will I simply fall—one of many
shrieking in the light that chars
the sinners in a shriveled sky?

Will I find the old myths true: Angels, judgment,
a black pit—and for a few the marvelous
blue light that widens upward like a hand?

Believers rising as if shaken
out of sleep in the colors of Heaven.
And none of it mine.

No tool. No sign. No hill of words
that I could make or rake away
to level the mistake of disbelief.

CONQUEST

When it is done, the women live in the surges,
the dark that changes like a tide
as if refusing to demolish or decide.
They know the loss is a pact with the shore.

The colors here are crossed and banging,
old carpets hung among their dusts.
The sorrow around them visible as flour,
swatted by those whose time and thought don't matter.

Each bolt of cloth is retroactive, angry.
It falls downward, opens crookedly
the repeating blue-white lightning
and the thought of the shore.

They who are angry grow clumsy,
large, black, raucous birds
who rock on bent legs
in the brown stubble.

They call and complain of the lost,
the wind that was meant
to carry them all intact.
They remember the shore they love.

The shore revised with knowledge.

THE DEAD

The world they recall is window,
a clear dream where creatures fall.
Where rain lands hard, breaks
dark earth with the color of stars.

What is lost accrues as light,
pools alive with shape and wind.
A white loaf made of stillness,
a decay that makes it grow.

The dead resound without a word.
Let them go around you as music does,
toward the farther views
bright as the curves of horses.

Ask the dead the word for horse.
The word will be blue and gray,
wide and smooth, a mesa.
A ground that shakes.

Its gallop strikes the freshness
of this silence like a wild rain,
gusts of brown where colors cannot go,
a listening as deep as sobbing.

GRIEF SONG

In this wild place your grief
blows like a burning of sand
and the wind makes marks upon it.

The straight, starved line of the wind
leaves beauty upon beauty
in the weight and the enormity.

Go forward as wanderers do.
The edges of your soul
will toughen or burn away.

Walk until you are burning too,
until you are gray and know
you are empty.

MUSHROOMS

Picking mushrooms at the edge of dread
—Adrienne Rich

Go to the soundless mushrooms,
still, cool moons in the black earth:
The low and loaf-white forest
growing in a vast, strange shade.

Far from the thrumming light,
the work you walk through,
your task that disentangles
you from nothingness.

Maybe there's a small dark flower
in your forehead, made of quiet—
ancient, simple, creased
from leaning on your dreaming.

Small lights smelling of the forest,
moth-pale and folded
through the fluttering transom
or under the dark door.

How patient that light is,
holding the silent, dreamt things:
the buried silver, bent in the rock,
soft snail swallowing a gray night.

THE MYTHICAL ANIMAL

The animal was massive.
His skin the color of twilight
under the black of his hair.
He waylaid us with his eye
and the flowering horn on his nose.

With his little hooves he carried
the heavy, widening view
as sinners do, like a correction.
He dragged its blues and yellows
into the dark of everywhere.

Stand on his hoof prints and look up.
See the moon where the darks
are soft and glide like blossoms.
Or see the darkness whole: black air
that twists out lightning or a god.

GIANT

He walks upon the world
as if it were a line, a black one
without width or nuance.

Along the axis of the town,
he steps among the hot and small
who do not love his tall, black eye.

They think the giant watches them,
rakes them with his rank looks,
tastes them with dark wishes.

That he wants to pull them up
like roots or the corners of tents
and carry them away.

But the giant's eye is rapt and upward,
in a snow of slow, cold stars, a dark
that he lifts gently, like the water in his cup.

It's only the small who grab at strangeness,
run toward it with loud, ringing feet,
bringing a realization and a death.

WHAT WORD?

What word is deepest and most wished,
sinking its shadow in the dark rocks
squeezing the river of its shape?

Which thought has dried and gone,
invisible as sky to the long animal
with tall, blue, moving eyes?

Where is his smoke-thin dream,
signing the air with its smallness
like an insect's gray and trailing hands?

His thoughts in the dark
are bright as a wing or rake.
A racket of small, white stones.

A voice that is in us, or about us.
Pale and cold around us,
pushing like the river.

A memory of light: large birds
raising the rickety rack of flight,
that faint afterimage, floating.

HOOK FOR THE MASTERPIECE

The weight of line and shade still hangs.
A frame holds the glow they made of it:
The kingdom of smoking fuels,
the art with its light-craving dervish.

Women made of shadow and the world.
Brown rats that squeaked and bit them.
Crowns of dead metal stamens. Fevers
or sainthood that might seize them like a light.

On the wall a battle empties like a sunset:
Angels, eyes-up bodies, devils wafting.
A king's win burning,
stinking of its need to be visible.

We who are far from the battle lean toward it
like sails white with belief.
Saints with a stir of shine on our heads,
a smolder of dawn on our palms.

The Garden and the Thorns

—Pony Ride, a painting by Horst Gottschalk

The light in the garden holds a boy
and the stillness of a small white horse.
The boy wears a feather in his hat and turns
the small blue circles of his eyes.

Beyond the circle of color and light
is the unkempt dark of fir and thorns—
a strangeness, a tilt as of hills
or the marks where the sea wave went
that lifts and bends its creatures.

And knowing, which is also strange—and cold.
The black where wishes rise like swarms.
The shadow that bolts when you mount it
with your jaunty little hat.

About the Author

Patricia Nelson is a retired attorney and environmentalist. She has worked with the "Activist" group of poets in California for many years. The Activist credo is that every word in a poem should be poetically "active," employing some kind of highly focused poetic technique—a principle not as self-evident as it might sound. The group, which formed in the 1930s around Lawrence Hart, might also be described as neo-Modernists. The first generation of poets taught by Hart rose to prominence in the 1940s and 50s and the group subsequently fell out of fashion. The "Activists" are now experiencing a resurgence of publication by a different generation of poets. Among the group's signature techniques are clusters of intense metaphoric imagery and a preference for associational, rather than narrative organization.

www.ingramcontent.com/pod-product-compliance
Lightning Source LLC
Chambersburg PA
CBHW081332090426
42737CB00017B/3108